What If It Was All a Lie?

And What Happens When You Remember the Truth

By

Chicole Hedgebeth Powell

This book is a work of non-fiction based on the author's personal experiences, reflections, and interpretations. The content is intended for informational and inspirational purposes only and should not be considered a substitute for professional advice.

First Edition

Printed in the United States of America ISBN: 979-8-234-05145-5

Cover Design: Amir N

Publisher: *Chicole Hedgebeth Powell*

www.chicolesworld.com

For those who are awakening.

For every soul who has ever felt the quiet whisper
that there must be more — this book is for you.

May it remind you of what you've always known
deep down:

You were never broken. You were always divine.

"And it is so."

Note from the Author

Thank you for holding this book in your hands. This isn't just a book—it's a piece of my journey, shared with you in the hope that it stirs something in your Spirit. Writing these words was more than an act of storytelling; it was an act of remembrance. If this book has shifted something in you—even in the smallest way—I want you to know it's only the beginning. Awakening is not a one-time moment; it's a continual unfolding.

I invite you to read these words slowly. Sit with them. Let them resonate in your body. Question them, if you must. And when they call you to, return to them again and again.

If this message has moved you, I'd love to connect further. Visit me at www.chicolesworld.com, subscribe to my YouTube Channels Chicoles World or listen to my podcast, *She Shifted: The Mindset Makeover,* where I continue these conversations on mindset, belief, and spiritual alignment.

Because together, as we remember who we are, we
shift the world.
With love and deep gratitude,
Chicole Hedgebeth Powell
And IT IS SO.

Table of Contents

Introduction

What If I Told You It Was All Lies?

What if I told you that everything we've been taught — from the moment we were born — was a lie? Aging, religion, sickness, struggle, lack, separation — all of it.

We didn't just inherit skin and blood; we inherited programs — beliefs passed down through generations, institutions, and well-meaning people who never realized they were repeating a spell. We were told what to believe about time, health, and what's "normal," and we accepted it. We believed it. And so, it became real.

Here's the truth: reality bends to belief. Belief isn't fact — it's agreement. And when enough people agree on something, it becomes the norm. But what happens when you stop agreeing? What happens when one soul decides to stop running the same tired code and remembers the truth it knew before the world taught it otherwise?

This is not a book of theories or recycled spiritual fluff. It's a transmission. A wake-up call. I'm not here to teach you something new. I'm here to help you remember what your Spirit already knows: you were never meant to decay, to suffer, or to die small.

You came here to expand, to radiate, to live in divine alignment, and to heal the field through your belief.

This book won't speak over your head. It will speak to your cells, your soul, and that quiet voice within that has always whispered, "There has to be more than this." There is. And it begins with unlearning everything they told you was true.

Chapter One

The Lie you were born into

This will be challenging on many levels. For some, it may feel like betrayal. For others, it will feel like liberation. Either way, it will make you feel—and that's how you know the unlearning has begun.

Most of us grew up wholeheartedly believing what we were told—not because we researched it, and not because it made sense, but because it came from people we trusted. We believed our parents, pastors, teachers, doctors, and even the news. They never meant to mislead us. They loved us. And when you're young, love and truth often feel the same.

But what if they weren't? What if our parents, preachers, and teachers were simply passing down beliefs they never questioned themselves? This doesn't make them bad; it makes them human. Lies wrapped in love feel like truth, and that's what makes this process so hard. You're not just questioning information—you're questioning identity, memory, tradition, and the very foundation you were built on.

For those with deep religious roots, this can feel like blasphemy. It sounds like rebellion, disrespect, or even danger. But that fear is exactly what was taught: that questioning is sin, that curiosity is rebellion, that God is fragile, and that faith means never doubting.

I can remember a time when my husband and I would get into deep conversations about Jesus. To him, the stories were just that — stories. He believed we weren't supposed to be praying to a man at all. To me, hearing that felt dangerous. Not just disagreeable — **dangerous***.*

I remember thinking, This is blasphemy. My mind raced to all the things I'd been taught about what happens to people who reject Jesus. I told myself silently — and sometimes out loud — that I would not go to hell for what he believed. I felt certain my faith had carried me to this point in my life, had protected me, had opened doors. I wasn't about to risk losing that because my husband saw things differently.

In my heart, I believed we were unequally yoked. I even convinced myself that certain things weren't happening for me — blessings I thought I deserved — because of his lack of belief. And there was one thought that lodged itself in my mind and wouldn't leave: Don't stand too close to him during a thunderstorm. As irrational as it sounds now, I truly felt we might get struck down together, simply because he didn't see Jesus the way I did.

Here's what I've learned: God is not offended by your questions. God is the question. The Divine isn't afraid of your awakening — it has been waiting for it. Think about it: why would we fear the Source we call on for healing? Why would we tremble before the same God we beg to save our loved ones or protect us? Why would the One we trust for grace punish us for using the very mind and voice It gave us?

Truth doesn't fear inspection. The Creator isn't fragile. Real faith isn't silent; it's connected. You were born curious. That wasn't sin – that was sacred design.

Reflection Exercise – The Collision of Love & Lies

Think of one belief you inherited from someone you love deeply – parent, spouse, pastor, or mentor – that you've never questioned.

1. *Write it down, exactly as you were taught to believe it.*
2. *Beside it, write where it came from and who taught it to you.*
3. *Now ask yourself: Do I believe this because it's true for me, or because I love and respect the person who passed it down?*
4. *If it no longer feels aligned, write one small question you can begin exploring without judgment.*

You are not betraying them by questioning. You are honoring the truth by seeking it.

Chapter Two
The Change — How to Begin

Unlearning the Lie

There comes a moment — after the whisper, after the question, after that inner shake — when you realize you can't go back to sleep. You felt it in Chapter One: the questions began, the discomfort stirred, and the permission to examine what you once held sacred was granted. Whether you admit it out loud or not, something has shifted.

This is where the change begins.

Unlearning is not forgetting. Unlearning is the conscious decision to release what no longer fits your Spirit. It is the sacred unraveling of the story you were handed, so you can write the one your soul came here to live.

So, where do we start?

We start with awareness. We start by seeing the lie for what it is: a belief, not a fact. We begin by recognizing that repetition, tradition, and authority don't make something true. When we admit that truth is bigger than any doctrine, diagnosis, or dogma, we finally make space for something new.

Let me share my story.

Since I can remember—from birth, really—I was in church. My dad was a bishop, and my grandfather had been a pastor who even owned his own church. My foundation wasn't just spiritual; it was deeply religious, rooted in generations of belief. We followed tradition to the letter. I had to wear skirts. We weren't allowed to spend the night out. We couldn't listen to anything but gospel music.

At the time, I thought it was about rules. Now, I understand it was about protection — mental, emotional, and spiritual. My dad didn't want our minds distracted by the outside world. He wanted to guard our thoughts before they had a chance to wander. He was controlling, yes, but I see now that it came from fear — fear rooted in what he was taught. In his heart, he only wanted the best for us.

That's when I realized: even those who love us deeply can pass down programs that limit our freedom — not out of harm, but out of habit, love, fear, and tradition. Unlearning doesn't dishonor them; it frees both of us.

***Years later**, a book called Outwitting the Devil by Napoleon Hill shook me in an entirely new way. I can remember how I felt when the words hit my soul — especially the part where he spoke about what children should be taught. Me, being a mother of five, immediately felt my thinking go into overdrive. I realized I had it mixed up. I was raising them the way I had been taught, and I hadn't even noticed it because of the programming I had been* *given. That book made me face the fact that I was unconsciously passing down the same conditioning that I had spent my adult life trying to unlearn. From that moment on, I knew I had to change.*

Unlearning requires three things: curiosity, courage, and consistency.

Curiosity: The First Crack in the Code

Curiosity is not rebellion; it's the first step toward freedom. Children are born curious. We asked "why" long before anyone told us we shouldn't. Jesus even said in Matthew 18:3, "Truly I tell you, unless you change and become like little children, you will never enter the kingdom of heaven." What if He was pointing us back to curiosity, wonder, and openness?

When we ask, we activate. When we seek, we find. Yet we were conditioned to believe questions were dangerous. Science told us what was, religion told us what to fear, and culture told us what was acceptable. But the truth is still yours to discover.

Courage: The Energy to Let Go

Unlearning means you will lose some things. Maybe not all at once, but gently, piece by piece. It might mean releasing beliefs that once made you feel safe but now keep you small. It might mean letting go of religious rules that taught you to fear your own body, or scientific claims that dismissed the unseen, or cultural norms that shamed your intuition.

It takes courage to let go of beliefs that once protected you. What protected you then may now be limiting you. John 8:32 says, "And you shall know the truth, and the truth shall make you free." But freedom requires courage. You must be willing to walk out of the prison — even when the door has been open all along.

Consistency: The Daily Practice of Remembering
Unlearning is not a one-time event; it's a daily practice. You'll question something, replace it with truth, and then feel yourself drift back into old beliefs. That's normal. Every day, you must choose: will I believe what they told me, or will I believe what I now know?

Romans 12:2 reminds us, "Do not conform to the pattern of this world, but be transformed by the renewing of your mind." Renewing your mind isn't a single moment — it's an ongoing movement.

Here's a simple practice:

Write down a belief you were taught (e.g., "I must age and decline"). Ask yourself: Who told me this? Where did they learn it? Then ask: What do I believe now? Replace it with: "I am designed to regenerate. I live in divine alignment with vitality and truth." Repeat it. Speak it. Feel it in your body. Watch your reality begin to shift.

*In the chapters ahead, we will break down major belief systems —
aging, illness, religion, and science — and show you how to
unlearn them step by step. For now, remember: the change begins
with a question. The question leads to truth. And the truth will
lead you home.*

Chapter Three
It Was Never Real: Frequency, Belief & the Power of Agreement

By now, something in you has shifted. The questions have been asked. The unlearning has begun. And yet, you may feel like you're in a tug-of-war between what you've always believed and what you now sense deep within.

This is one of the hardest parts of the journey, because what if the very thing you're clinging to is the very thing holding you back?

What if belief itself — the thing you thought anchored you — is actually the barrier?

This chapter is for the strongest believers: those who have anchored their entire identity in science, religion, tradition, or culture. The ones who say, "This is just how life works." "This is what the body does." "This is what the Bible says." "This is what science proves."

*But here's the question: **What if belief is the filter?** What if you're not seeing truth — you're only seeing through your belief?*

Belief Is a Code, Not the Truth

Your beliefs live in your subconscious. You don't see them — you see through them. They color how you interpret pain, aging, illness, miracles, and even God. The subconscious doesn't know the difference between truth and repetition. It simply accepts what it's told, especially when it's reinforced by emotion or authority.

If you've been told the body deteriorates with age, you believe it. If you've been told God only loves you if you obey certain rules, you believe it. If you've been told energy isn't real because it can't be measured in a lab, you believe that too.

But just because something is widely accepted, measured, or worshiped doesn't make it ultimate truth. It only makes it agreed upon.

Belief is like a code written in invisible ink across the lens of your mind. It determines what you notice, what you ignore, what you call "real," and what you label "impossible." Some codes serve us, while others silently sabotage us. Most of them, we didn't even write — they were installed before we were old enough to choose.

When belief becomes too rigid, it stops being faith and starts becoming a cage. It traps you inside its logic. It convinces you that freedom is rebellion, that curiosity is danger, and that new understanding is betrayal. But faith was never meant to trap — it was meant to expand.

For years, I believed I had to prove myself to be seen as valuable — as a wife, a mother, and even in business. I thought I had to constantly do to be worthy of rest, love, or abundance. That belief ran so deep I didn't even recognize it as one; it just felt like "the right way to be."

Then one day, I was sitting at my desk, overwhelmed by everything I thought I had to finish to "earn" peace. I was checking boxes, answering messages, thinking about dinner, homeschool, content — everything all at once — when a quiet thought came in and interrupted it all:

"What if nothing's missing? What if you already are?"

It stopped me cold. I realized how many years I had spent striving for alignment while already living in it. I had been manifesting from lack, not love. That moment showed me that my belief in not being enough was the only thing separating me from peace.

The next day, I did something radical — I didn't rush. I moved slower. I trusted that alignment doesn't require effort, only awareness. And everything shifted.

That was the moment I truly understood: sometimes the belief that you still have to "get there" is the barrier keeping you from realizing you already are.

The Power of Frequency (And What They Never Taught Us)

At the foundation of everything in existence is frequency. This isn't just spiritual language – it's physics. Everything vibrates. Everything has resonance. You. Your thoughts. Your emotions. Your beliefs.

Think of a moment when you were in love, at peace, or overflowing with joy. That tingling feeling in your body? That was high frequency.

I felt this deeply the morning I truly awakened. The very questions I now write about surged through me, but this time, they came with knowing – with certainty. It felt undeniable.

That morning, my frequency was so high that it brought tears to my eyes. It was a rush of remembrance. I felt it again when I decided to write this book. It was like my Spirit declared: This is it. This is the message. That high frequency affirmed that I wasn't imagining it – I was remembering.

Fear lowers your frequency. Love raises it. What you believe determines where you vibrate – and what you attract.

Jesus didn't just heal people; He said, "Your faith has made you well." Belief shifted frequency, and frequency transformed the body.

Modern science quietly echoes this truth. Dr. Bruce Lipton, author of The Biology of Belief, showed how thoughts and emotions literally change our cells. When we shift our internal energy, the body follows suit. That's not metaphor — it's measurable biology.

When you hold a thought of fear, your body releases cortisol and contracts. When you hold a thought of peace, your cells expand and your immune system strengthens. The difference between fear and faith is frequency.

Nature: Our Greatest Teacher

When you're ready to unlearn, go outside. Look at the trees. They don't fear time. Birds don't wake up anxious. A lion doesn't doubt its identity. Flowers don't bloom wondering who's watching.

Nature simply is. It trusts. It regenerates.
Some trees live thousands of years. A lizard can grow back its tail. Certain jellyfish can reverse aging altogether. Yet we — who call ourselves the most "intelligent" species — accept decay as inevitable because we were told it's "natural."

We saw our parents age, get sick, and die, and because everyone around us agreed, we never questioned it. Until now.

The next time you're in nature, take off your shoes. Feel the ground beneath you. Notice how the earth doesn't rush. How the wind doesn't explain itself. How the river doesn't ask for permission to flow. That's the frequency of trust. That's what remembering feels like.

The Mirror of Belief

If frequency is energy in motion, belief is the pattern that energy follows. Change the pattern, and everything else rearranges itself.

This is why manifestation doesn't work when your beliefs don't match your desires. You can affirm abundance all day, but if you still believe you're unworthy, the vibration you send out says lack.

To shift reality, you must shift belief — not just on the surface, but in the subconscious where your codes are written. That's where the real transformation begins.

The body listens to the mind. The mind listens to the heart. The heart listens to belief.

And belief listens to the one voice you often silence: your own truth.

What Now?

This isn't about discarding everything you've ever believed. It's about asking:

Is my belief keeping me alive — or just keeping me safe?

Sometimes what feels safe to the mind is the most dangerous thing for the soul.

Belief isn't bad, but it should never go unchallenged. You're not here to blindly repeat inherited agreements. You're here to remember what's real beyond the programming.

So sit with this:

What if your beliefs were never really yours?

And what would happen if you chose new ones?

Reflection Exercise – Breaking the Code

1. *Write down one belief you've held as "absolute truth."*
2. *Ask yourself: Where did this belief come from? Who benefits from me keeping it?*
3. *Close your eyes, breathe deeply, and imagine that belief as a wall. What happens when you take a brick out of it?*
4. *Now write a new belief — one that feels free, expansive, and aligned.*

5. *Speak it out loud. Feel how your body responds. That's frequency shifting.*

Chapter Four
The Truth About Aging — You Were Never Meant to Decay

By the time most people reach adulthood, they have already accepted aging as a slow surrender. Wrinkles, pain, fatigue, decline — we are taught to expect these things as a normal part of life. The messaging is so constant, so repetitive, so emotionally charged, that we rarely question it.

But what if aging — as we've been taught to understand it — isn't a biological certainty, but a psychological agreement?

What if the body doesn't actually break down because of time, but because of belief?

You are not the same person you were when you first began this journey.

Your awareness has expanded.

Your Spirit has taught you what the world never could.

And one truth rises above them all:

Aging is not a punishment — it is a state of consciousness. And consciousness can shift.

This chapter is not about denying the body. It is about remembering what the body truly is: a responsive, intelligent, energetic instrument of awareness. Not a machine destined to rust, but a living expression of the Spirit inhabiting it.

The Programming of Decline

From early childhood, we hear it:

- *"That's what happens when you get older."*
- *"Enjoy your youth while it lasts."*
- *"Our bodies fall apart after a certain age."*
- *"It's all downhill from here."*

These phrases come from people who loved you — parents, grandparents, teachers — so you swallowed them without question. Over time, they became subconscious commands. Not facts. Not truth. Just repeated beliefs disguised as destiny.

But think about this:

If humans were designed to fall apart…

Why is the body constantly fighting to stay alive?

Why does the heart correct itself?
Why do cells divide and replace themselves?

Why does the body regenerate after injury?

Why do bones fuse and mend?

Why does the immune system adapt to every threat it meets?

The body is always regenerating — unless the mind commands otherwise.

Modern research now confirms a spiritual truth humanity forgot: **your belief about your body becomes instruction to your body.**

Your biology follows your expectation, not your age.

Your Spirit Already Knows the Truth

There is a knowing within you that has nothing to do with science or tradition — a knowing that whispers that you were never created to decline. That your cells respond to your consciousness. That your body listens to your emotions, your words, your energy, and your identity.

You have likely felt this already.
Maybe in a moment of peace when you felt ageless. Maybe during a spiritual awakening, when your body felt weightless.

Maybe after releasing an old emotion and noticing your body shift instantly.

Maybe when joy made you feel younger. Maybe when stress made you feel older.

Your Spirit has been showing you the truth all along:
Your body takes shape according to how you live inside it.

The world taught you to fear time. Your Spirit is teaching you to master it.

A Moment That Changed My Understanding of Aging

There came a moment in my own life when this realization hit me.

I was listening to people around me talk about their bodies as if decline was guaranteed. Each ache became "proof" of getting older. Each birthday a reminder. Each new line on the face a sign that youth was leaving.

I found myself repeating the same lines, not because I believed them, but because they were familiar — the same way children repeat their parents' language before understanding the meaning.

One day, I heard myself say it:

"That's just what happens when you get older." But

something in my Spirit disagreed.

It wasn't loud.

It was quiet.

Certain.

Steady.

It asked me one simple question that shook everything:

Who told you that?

That question unraveled the entire agreement.

Because if aging is truly natural, why do some people stay youthful their entire lives? Why do some people glow at 50, 60, 70, while others feel old at 30? Why do joy, peace, purpose, and alignment reverse physical symptoms in people every day?

What if the difference isn't time — but consciousness?

Nature Reveals the Truth About Regeneration

Look at the earth:

Trees regenerate bark.

Starfish grow back limbs.

Deer regrow antlers.

Certain jellyfish reverse their aging cycle.

Human skin renews every few weeks.

The stomach lining renews every few days.

Your bones rebuild in cycles.

Your blood forms new blood every 120 days.

If decay were the destiny, regeneration would not be built into everything.

Life renews itself constantly.
Only humans believe renewal stops.

Animals don't fear aging.
Grass doesn't fear growing back.
Ocean waves don't fear returning.
The sun doesn't fear rising.

Everything in nature trusts rebirth.

The Biology of Belief and the Aging of the Mind

Science is now catching up to what your Spirit always knew:

- *Stress accelerates aging*
- *Fear collapses the body*
- *Anger inflames the system*

- *Shame shuts down cell repair*
- *Trauma freezes the body in time*
- *Joy expands and regenerates*
- *Peace slows biological aging*
- *Identity signals the body how to behave*

Your body follows the mind.
Your mind follows belief.
Belief follows identity.
Identity follows consciousness.

Which means aging isn't a number — it's
a level of awareness.

You age according to what you are aligned with, not how many
birthdays you've had.

Aging as a Frequency, Not a Fate

When you awaken, something shifts.

You stop identifying with your body and
start aligning with your being.

You stop counting years and
start measuring vibration.

You stop fearing time   and
start remembering truth.

Aging stops being a countdown. and
becomes a choice.
 A state.
 A frequency.
 A consciousness.

Some people feel alive at 60.
 Some feel exhausted at 30.

It has nothing to do with age —
everything to do with alignment. This
doesn't mean the body doesn't change.

Because it does.

Hair may turn gray.
Skin may shift.
The body may reflect time in visible ways.

Those are natural changes.

But change…
is not the same as decline.

We were taught to associate aging with
deterioration.
With slowing down.
With losing vitality.

And that belief...

is what many people actually embody.

Not because it's absolute truth.

But because it's been accepted as truth.

So the body follows the belief.

What Now? Rewriting the Agreement

Ask yourself:

Who taught me that aging is decline?
Why did I accept it?
What would happen if I didn't?
Who would I become if I stopped expecting decay?
What would my body look like if I trusted its intelligence?

You were never meant to decay.
You were meant to remember.

You were meant to regenerate.

You were meant to choose your state of being.

And you can choose again — right now.

Reflection Exercise: Renewing the Body Through Consciousness

1. *Write down every belief you were taught about aging.*
2. *Circle the ones that no longer resonate.*
3. *Ask: Do these beliefs align with who I am today?*
4. *Cross out every belief you choose to release.*
5. *Write one new belief that feels alive, expansive, and true.*
6. *Speak it out loud until your body responds.*

Your cells are listening.

Your consciousness is leading.

Your body will follow.

Chapter Five
Leaving the Agreement — How to Exit the World's Normal

Belief doesn't have to be true to be powerful – it just has to be shared.

That's how "normal" is created.

We agree that aging is inevitable.
We agree that some diseases are incurable.
We agree that decline is unavoidable.
We agree that fear is wisdom.
We agree that struggle is necessary.
We agree that suffering is holiness.

And so… it becomes reality.

Not because it is true.
But because it has been repeated for so long that the collective stops questioning it. But here's the truth:

"Normal" is nothing more than a shared agreement.
And you can step out of it at any time.
You don't have to subscribe to society's script.
You don't have to move in rhythm with the world's limitations.
You don't have to accept beliefs that were handed to you before you had the wisdom to choose.

You can choose your own truth.

You can create your own outcomes.

You can leave the agreement.

My Brother's Words

My brother Abraham once told me something I'll never forget.

Our relationship had been strained; his energy toward me felt distant. I couldn't read him. I didn't understand him. And honestly, at times, I thought I had done something wrong.

Then one day, he looked at me and said,
"It's not you. It's what I saw. I kept my distance because I didn't want to interfere with what I knew you were going to do."

Those words etched themselves into my soul.
He had seen something in me before I could see it myself.
He witnessed the calling before I accepted it.
He sensed the assignment before I stepped into it.

Even through jealousy, confusion, distance — his truth was clear:
He knew.
And now…
I know too.

Just the other day, I felt overwhelmed by joy, love, peace, gratitude — everything at once. It was divine remembrance. Something ancient. Something holy. I felt chosen by the Creator to deliver this message. My body could barely hold it. I gagged — not from sickness — but because my Spirit was making space for purpose.

The same girl who once shrank herself to keep peace,
who buried her words in journals, who waited for permission,
who dimmed her light so others wouldn't feel small — she was gone.

Because now I know:
They saw it before I did.
And now that I see it, nothing will ever be the same.

The Eagle Story — Remembering Who You Are

There's a story that speaks to this moment, a story that mirrors what it feels like to leave the world's agreement.

A farmer once found an eagle's egg and placed it in a chicken coop. When it hatched, the eagle lived among chickens, believing it was one of them.
It scratched the ground.
It pecked at food.
It never looked up.

Every day, it watched the other birds fly overhead,
but because everyone around it stayed grounded, it
believed it was meant to stay grounded too.

One day, a real eagle soared above the farm.
 The young eagle froze, mesmerized.
 There was something familiar about that bird — something that
stirred remembrance.

The chickens said, "Don't
look at that bird.
 Don't desire the sky.
We don't fly.
We stay here, on the ground."
And so the young eagle lowered its head.
 It returned to its small life.
 It believed the agreement.

Until one day, it heard a voice — from the eagle above — calling,
"Look up.
This is what you were always meant to be."

Something inside the young eagle awakened.
 Something ancient.
 Something undeniable.

And in that moment... it
leapt.

It spread its wings.
It remembered.

The eagle didn't become something new — it
became what it always was.

The world had mistaken it.
But the truth had not changed.

This is the story of leaving the agreement: **You don't**
become someone else — you return to the one you were
before the programming.

Leaving the Agreement

When you decide to leave the world's agreement, you will feel it.

You may feel judged.
You may feel mocked.
You may feel alone.
You may feel misunderstood.
You may feel like something inside you is breaking.

But that "breaking" is actually remembering. You are
breaking out of the illusion so you can become who you
were always meant to be.

*The world will not understand you at first — because
you are no longer speaking in its language.*

You will stop repeating its beliefs.
You will stop shrinking into its comfort.
You will stop apologizing for your truth.
You will stop living by rules that were meant to keep you small.

*Your Spirit is calling you out of the old agreement and
into a higher one:*
 ***the agreement of truth, awareness, identity, and
embodiment.***

You don't have to believe in aging as they taught you.
You don't have to accept disease as fate.
You don't have to inherit your family's patterns.
You don't have to repeat your childhood programming.
You don't have to stay in the vibration of the collective.

You can choose differently.
You are choosing differently.
That is why you're reading these words right now.

Belief is energy.
One new belief can change your body.
One shift in frequency can change your diagnosis.
One awakened soul can transform the world.

When you leave the agreement, you become the proof that a new world is possible.

Reflection Exercise — Where Are You Still Agreeing?

1. *Write down every "truth" you've accepted because everyone else did.*

2. *Put a star next to the ones that no longer feel aligned.*

3. *Ask yourself: Who taught me this? Why did I believe it?*

4. *Draw a line through every belief you choose to leave behind today.*

5. *Write one new agreement that matches who you are remembering.*

Remember:

You are not breaking rules — you are breaking illusions.

Chapter Six
Frequency and Embodiment — The Energy That Shapes Reality

By now, you've seen the truth: beliefs shape biology and expectations shape experience. Now it's time to understand what ties it all together: frequency.

Frequency is the language of the universe.
It's the vibration you emit before you ever speak.
It's the silent signature that tells life what to bring you.

You don't attract what you want — you
attract what you are.

You can write affirmations until your wrists hurt, pray until your voice cracks, and visualize until you're dizzy... but if your frequency is misaligned, nothing sticks.

Because life responds to your energetic identity, not your intentions.

Action vs. Embodiment

Self-help often tells us to:

- *make vision boards*

- *write goals*

- *create routines*

- *take massive action*

And while action has its place, action alone will never shift your frequency.

Ever wonder why:

- *you can't stick to goals*

- *you fall back into old habits*

- *you start strong and then lose momentum*

- *your resolutions fade by February*

- *discipline feels like a battle*

It's not weakness.
It's not laziness.

It's not lack of willpower.

It's misalignment.

*Until your energy matches your desired outcome, you'll resist it.
Until your body holds the belief, you'll sabotage it. Until
you become the frequency of what you want, you will chase
instead of receive.*

*I've struggled with my weight since high school. I'm 43 now. For
the first time, I see why change didn't stick before: it wasn't
about diet or exercise. It was about who I was **being**.*

*On the inside, I still identified with struggle.
I saw myself trying, not transformed.
I moved as someone who hoped — not someone who embodied.*

*The day I shifted my frequency — when I became the version of me
who felt whole and free — everything changed.
Habits shifted naturally.
My cravings disappeared.
The scale moved.
But more importantly, I did.
Because when your frequency changes, reality follows.*

What Is Energetic Embodiment?

*Energetic embodiment is becoming the version of yourself you desire to be — **now**.*

Before the money comes.
Before the healing appears.
Before the relationship changes.
Before the career manifests.

You shift your energy first.

You speak, think, feel, and move as if it's already done — because in the unseen realm where all outcomes exist, it is.

This is why:

- *vision boards don't work by themselves*

- *affirmations fall flat*

- *journaling feels repetitive*

- *manifestation seems inconsistent*

- *change doesn't "stick"*

Energy doesn't lie.

*Your mouth can say one thing, but
your vibration reveals the truth.*

*When your body doesn't believe it, your
life won't receive it.*

Embodiment is when your body becomes the prayer.

A Personal Moment of Embodiment

*There was a morning when I woke up and felt different.
Not lighter.
Not smaller.
Not physically changed.*

But energetically transformed.

*It was subtle, but real.
Something within me had shifted into alignment with the version
of myself I had been trying to "remember."
For the first time, I wasn't hoping for change — I
was change.*

*I stood differently.
I spoke differently.
I moved differently.
I made choices from a different level of consciousness.*

*Not because I forced discipline, but
because I embodied a new identity.*

That day, I realized:
 **the body follows the mind, and
the mind follows frequency.**

Frequency Doesn't Wait for Evidence

One of the biggest traps in transformation is waiting for proof.

*Waiting for the scale to move.
 Waiting for the business to grow.
 Waiting for the relationship to improve.
 Waiting for the opportunity to show up.
But frequency doesn't wait.
 Frequency doesn't need evidence.
 Frequency doesn't ask permission.*

*You shift first.
 Reality adjusts second.*

*Your embodiment is the signal.
 Your future responds to your frequency.*

Embodiment Is Not Pretending

People misunderstand embodiment and think it means "fake it until you make it."

But embodiment is not pretending.
Pretending feels empty.
Embodiment feels true.

Pretending comes from insecurity.
Embodiment comes from remembrance.

Pretending says,
"I hope this works."

Embodiment says,
"It already has."
Pretending creates tension.
Embodiment creates ease.

The Invitation to Remember

If you want to:

- *release what no longer serves you*

- *reach your goals*

- *transform your relationships*

- *heal your body*

- *break old patterns*

- *elevate your life*

- *live in alignment*

It begins here:

Frequency first.
Ask yourself:

"Who is the version of me that already has this?" *Then*

ask deeper:

- *What do they believe?*

- *How do they walk?*

- *How do they speak?*

- *What does he or she no longer accept?*

- *What boundaries do they hold?*

- *What habits come naturally to him or her?*

- *What do they expect from life?*

- *What does she or he not tolerate anymore?*

Then — you embody
them now.

Not tomorrow.
Not when the evidence shows up.
Not when you feel ready.

Now.

Change doesn't begin with doing more.
*It begins with **being different**.*

When your frequency aligns, action becomes
effortless, opportunities become obvious, and
life reshapes itself around your identity.

*Because the universe responds to one thing only: **who** **you are being.***

Reflection Exercise — Becoming the Frequency

1. *Write down one area of your life you want to transform.*

2. *Describe — in detail — the version of you who already has it.*

3. *Circle three characteristics she embodies daily.*

4. *Choose one and practice it today, in your body, not just your mind.*

5. *Notice what shifts — even subtly — when you inhabit her energy.*

You are not trying to become the person you're meant to be.
You already are that person.
Your only job is to remember.

Chapter Seven
Protecting the Frequency — How to Stay Aligned in a Low-Vibe World

Now that you've recalibrated your beliefs and shifted your frequency, a new challenge emerges staying aligned. Transformation is not a single moment. It's not the morning you feel awakened or the night you fall to your knees in remembrance. Awakening is easy. **Maintenance is mastery.**

Modern life — through technology, media, distractions, and even well-meaning relationships — can drown out your signal with noise.

And the truth about noise is this:

It doesn't always show up loudly.

It doesn't always announce itself.

Sometimes it comes quietly, slipping in through routine, familiarity, or habit.

This noise doesn't just distract; it pulls you back into old frequency patterns, subtly tugging you toward the beliefs you've been working hard to unlearn.

Noise reminds you of who you used to be.

Signal reminds you of who you truly are.

If you don't learn how to protect your frequency, the world will subtly teach you to lower it again.

"Being in the world but not of it."

Jesus said in John 15:19 (NLT):

> *"If the world hated you, keep in mind that it hated
> me first… it does not belong to the world any more
> than I belong to the world."*

Spiritual maturity doesn't mean escaping the world — it means **holding your frequency steady while moving through it.** *It means understanding that you can walk among people you love without absorbing their fear, their patterns, their distractive rhythms.*

You are here, but you are not from here.
You are a divine soul navigating a human realm.
You are consciousness housed in skin.

When you begin to live by energy and not just matter, you feel this truth deep within your being: alignment is not about isolation. It's about resonance. It's about choosing what you allow to influence your inner world. It's about deciding that nothing outside of you is more important than what God is doing inside you.

Being "in the world but not of it" becomes a lived experience — not a scripture you quote but a frequency you embody.

Signal vs. Noise: A Shift in My Spirit

I once heard Kevin O'Leary explain how Steve Jobs lived: "more signal, less noise."

The moment I heard those words, something in my Spirit responded. It wasn't inspiration – it was revelation.

I asked myself:

What is the noise in my life?

What is dimming my frequency?

What is pulling me back into the old agreement?

The answer came quickly.

Social media.

Mindless scrolling.

Unnecessary phone conversations.

People I cared about, but who carried chaos.

People who loved me, yet whose energy pressed on my Spirit in ways I could no longer ignore.

I could feel how every little distraction lowered me – just a few degrees at a time.

That's how noise works: slowly, subtly, quietly.

It doesn't knock you down.

It drains you.

It blurs you.

It takes your clarity one thought at a time.

So, I cleared it all.
I deleted every app.
I pulled my energy back.
I stopped trying to keep up with anything or anyone.

And in that silence, I heard God — not through thunder or prophecy, but through knowing so clear it felt like truth humming through my bones.

In the quiet, I remembered.
In the quiet, I felt guided.
In the quiet, I received the next instruction for my life.
In the quiet, I wrote this book.

Because in stillness, I found the signal again.

How to Protect Your Frequency

This world is loud, but you don't have to be.
It's chaotic, but you don't have to absorb it.
It's reactive, but you don't have to become reactionary.

You are allowed to live by a different rhythm — one that honors your soul instead of your schedule, your peace instead of your pressure, your truth instead of the world's noise.

Here is how you begin:

1.   Be intentional about input

Not everything deserves your attention.
Not every notification deserves your energy.
Not every message deserves your eyes.

Your attention is currency – spend it with discernment.

2.   Create sacred quiet

Stillness is not the absence of activity; it's the presence of alignment.
Turn off your phone.
Sit with your breath.
Let your mind settle long enough to hear yourself again.
The world calls silence "doing nothing." But
spiritually, silence is a portal.

3.   Choose alignment over distraction

Not every message needs a reply.
Not every call deserves answering.
Not every invitation is for you.

You are allowed to decline what disturbs your peace.

4.   Guard your gates

Your eyes.

Your ears.

Your mind.

Your Spirit.

You are the gatekeeper.

Filter what you allow in.

Everything you consume becomes part of your frequency.

5.   Ask daily: "Is this feeding my frequency or draining it?"

Your Spirit will answer instantly.

Your body will feel it.

Your energy will reveal it.

If it drains you, it is not for you in this season of elevation.

Your Invitation

This isn't about ignoring the world.

It's about discerning what adds to you and what subtracts.

*It's about choosing resonance over routine. It's
about remembering that your inner world is your
responsibility.*

*You are not rejecting people – you are returning to yourself.
You are not judging others – you are choosing alignment.
You are not isolating – you are elevating.*

*You are remembering how to be light **in** the noise without being
consumed **by** it.*

*Your frequency is holy.
Your clarity is sacred.
Your peace is your guidance system.
Your energy is your prayer.*

*When you protect them, everything changes.
For now, choose stillness.
Silence the noise.
Protect the signal.*

*Your energy is your message –
guard it with love, and walk in it
unapologetically.*

Chapter Eight The Power of Desire – Raising Your Frequency by Returning to Truth

There is a level of frequency that exists beyond effort, beyond action, and beyond the constant striving that so many of us were conditioned to believe was necessary for growth. It is not found in forcing, performing, or pushing yourself into spiritual exhaustion. Instead, it emerges through alignment – the quiet, intentional decision to return to the truth of who you have always been beneath the noise.

Alignment begins with one sacred recognition: that remembering yourself is more powerful than trying to become someone else. You don't need a candle, a ritual, or a carefully crafted mantra to access that remembering. You only need stillness – the kind of inner quiet where your breath is unhurried and your Spirit has enough space to speak.

Because somewhere inside you, there is already a knowing.
You know when you're in alignment because your body relaxes without asking permission.
You know when you're out of alignment because everything inside you tightens, contracts, or feels suddenly out of place.

Your Spirit is always speaking; it's simply overshadowed by the world's noise.

Frequency is not something you perform. It is something you inhabit.
It is the slow breath, the steady presence, and the internal clarity you carry even before you open your mouth.

And the shift begins with one phrase spoken honestly:
"I desire to be in truth."

Not want.
Not hope.
Not wish.
Desire.

Desire is intentional.
Desire is directional.
Desire says, "This already belongs to me, and I am now aligning with the version of myself who receives it." When desire is pure, it becomes a path.

From Longing to Embodiment

We've all said things like:

"I want to feel better."
"I want to lose weight."
"I want to leave this job."
"I want to grow this business."
"I want my life to change."

But wanting always places your transformation somewhere in the distance — in a future that only exists if circumstances align perfectly. Wanting rarely creates momentum because wanting comes from noticing what's missing. It keeps you attached to the feeling of lack.

Desire works differently.
Desire pulls the future into the present.
Desire is a spiritual memory — the soul reminding the mind of what is already real on a higher plane.

You don't manifest from longing or wishing.
You manifest from identity and alignment.
You manifest by remembering the version of yourself who already lives in the reality you desire to experience.

Desire is not yearning; desire is alignment.
It's the energetic shift from "I hope this happens" to "I am remembering who I am."

Truth Over Technique

Someone once told me, "Not all desires are healthy." I understood why he said that — he was speaking from a level of consciousness that had been taught to fear desire, to associate it with selfishness, lust, greed, or ego. Many people are conditioned to believe that wanting more is wrong, that wanting better is ungrateful, or that desire is dangerous.

But true desire — the kind that rises from the soul — is not ego. It is not greed. It is not the hunger of an empty spirit; it is the whisper of your higher self, revealing what you are meant to walk into.

Desire is not a craving — it is a calling.

I remember a period in my life when I tried spiritual techniques others swore by. People kept posting about how burning a white candle during meditation could open intuitive channels, deepen connection, or bring clarity. My desire at the time was clarity. So, I tried it. I bought the candle. I sat in silence. I prayed. I meditated. I waited.

But nothing happened.

Not because the ritual was wrong, but because it wasn't aligned with me.
There was no resonance.
There was no activation.

There was only quiet — and not the kind that brings revelation, but the kind that confirms, "This isn't your path."

That moment taught me something profound:
My truth will never come from mimicking someone else's method.
My clarity will come from stillness, from honesty, from breath, and from the direct connection between my Spirit and the Source that created it.

The deepest revelations of my life — including the vision and voice behind this book — didn't come from ritual. They came from remembering, from dreams, from sudden knowing, and from the moments where I finally stopped trying to force an experience and allowed myself to simply be present.

Alignment doesn't come from replication. It comes from recognition.

You recognize what resonates with you, and you release what doesn't — without guilt, judgment, or comparison.

Desire Reveals Your Direction

Desire is how your soul communicates with you.
It is the inward pull toward a future you have not lived yet but somehow remember.

It is the internal compass that guides you toward the version of yourself who already exists beyond fear and limitation.

When you desire peace, it's because peace is already inside you.
When you desire healing, it's because your body is ready to return to equilibrium.
When you desire transformation, it's because the next version of you is already forming within your consciousness.

Desire does not come from lack.
Desire comes from remembrance.

And remembrance always leads you home.

A Simple Practice

Here is one of the simplest yet most powerful ways to work with desire:

Sit in silence.
Close your eyes.
Allow your breath to deepen naturally.

Then speak softly, not from your mind but from your chest:
"I desire peace.

I choose peace.

I align with peace."

Don't rush through the words.
Feel each one.
Let your body register the frequency of what you're saying.
Let your energy shift as the truth settles inside you.

Repeat this whenever you feel pulled back into old habits, old patterns, or old beliefs about who you are allowed to remember.

When you move from true desire, you stop chasing alignment.
You start embodying it.

And when you become the frequency, your life begins to rearrange itself to match you.

What Comes Next

In the next chapter, we'll explore the body — not as an enemy you must dominate or punish, but as your divine messenger. You will learn to listen to it, honor it, and align with it in ways that create transformation from the inside out.

For now, hold this truth close:
Desire is divine.
Desire is direction.

And desire, aligned with truth, is the force that lifts you into the next version of yourself.

Chapter Nine The Body Remembers — Reclaiming the Divine Intelligence Within

We've unlearned the myths.

We've reclaimed the frequency.

Now we return to the vessel that has carried every version of you… your body.

This is the body that has been labeled too much, too soft, too dark, too loud, too heavy, too curvy, too visible, too wrong. It's the body you were taught to shrink, to hide, to fix, or to deny. It's the body religion told you was sinful, the body society tried to discipline, and the body science reduced to mere matter, ignoring the consciousness that animates it.

But this chapter is a homecoming not to your appearance, but to your awareness.

Because even when your mind was conditioned to forget your worth, your body never did.

Your body has always remembered what you truly are: divine, intelligent, responsive, and worthy of love.

Your body has been whispering truth long before you had the language to receive it.

The Body Is Not Your Enemy

*We live in a world that teaches us to fight our bodies, mistrust our signals, and ignore the messages that rise from within our own flesh. Yet what if your body has never betrayed you? What if every ache, craving, cycle, emotion, or pattern was never punishment, but **language**?*

Your body holds wisdom deeper than your thoughts.
It mirrors your emotions before you consciously recognize them.
It responds to your beliefs even when you pretend you don't have any.
It shifts with your frequency whether you acknowledge it or not.

The more your thoughts align with truth, the more your body reflects that alignment. Not through physical perfection, but through peace, regulation, and a settled nervous system.

Just as a tree bends naturally toward sunlight, your body leans toward whatever energy it is fed. When you speak life into it, it softens. When you listen to it, it answers. When you believe in its ability to heal, it begins reorganizing itself in ways science hasn't learned how to measure yet.

Your body is not an obstacle to overcome.
It is a messenger to interpret.
It is a partner in your evolution.
It is a mirror of your internal world.

And it has been waiting for you to come home.

Memory in the Flesh

In 2017, I had a moment that still lives in my body. My twin sister and I were getting ready for the Chris Brown "Party Tour," and I wanted to feel confident and beautiful in whatever I wore that night. I took myself to Old Navy, the store I believed was "safe" for me as a plus-sized woman, and began trying on outfits one after another.

Nothing was wrong with the clothes. But
something felt wrong inside me.

Then I tried on one particular outfit. It wasn't especially flattering. It wasn't transformative. It wasn't magical. But the moment I looked at myself in the dressing-room mirror, I froze. I stared at the woman looking back at me, and the tears formed before the thoughts did.

I didn't cry because I hated the outfit.
I cried because I finally felt the weight of how I had been
treating my body for years. Ignoring it, criticizing it, hiding it, punishing it, starving it of affection and attention.

As I stood there under those fluorescent lights, I realized my body had been loyal to me even when I had not been loyal to it. It carried me through pregnancies, heartbreaks, moves, stress, joy, and purpose. It held every version of me without complaint, without condition, without giving up on me.

That moment became a turning point.
I promised myself that I would learn to love and care for my body, not because someone told me to, not because society demanded it, and not because I wanted approval, but because **I desired to***. Because my body deserved the same love I freely gave to others.*

Our bodies hold memory.
They remember the years of silence.
They remember the moments of shame.
They remember the softness we tried to hide.
They remember the criticism spoken in private.
And they also remember the power that rises the moment we finally choose love.

This isn't about appearance.
It's about relationship.
It's about remembering who you are within the body you've been given.
And when you remember, your body responds with a clarity that feels like truth settling into your bones.

A Simple Practice

To return to your body, begin with presence:

1. Speak aloud:

*"You are divine. You are safe. You are loved." Let
your own voice become medicine.*

2. Stand in the mirror without judgment.

*Not to critique, not to compare, and not to fix.
Just to witness.
Just to love.*

3. Thank your body.

*Name the ways it has supported you.
Acknowledge what it has carried.
Honor what it has survived.*

4. Listen to it. Bless it. Partner with it.

*Your relationship with your body is the foundation of your
frequency.
When you honor it, it harmonizes with you.
The body remembers. And now... you
are learning to remember with it.*

Chapter Ten The Accident I Created — How Thought, Emotion, and Energy Became Reality

There are moments in life that split you open. Moments so sharp, so sudden, so undeniable that you cannot return to who you were before them. For me, one of those moments happened on March 19, 2011, on an ordinary day that was never meant to be ordinary at all. At the time, it felt like an accident, a random disruption in the flow of my life, a painful interruption I didn't ask for. But years later, when my awareness expanded and the truth began revealing itself layer by layer, I realized something that changed everything:

I created it.

Not consciously, not intentionally, not with malice but with energy, emotion, and belief I never knew I was emitting.

I understand now that nothing "just happens." Everything follows a vibration.
Everything matches a frequency.
Everything responds to the state of your inner world.

But back then, I didn't know any of this. I didn't understand manifestation, energetic laws, or the power of words. What I did understand deeply, painfully was longing. And longing is one of the most magnetic energies there is.

The Days Leading Up to the Accident

In the months before the accident, I was entangled in an emotional storm I didn't fully recognize. I had been writing in my journals, pouring out feelings I didn't know how to express aloud, trying to understand the ache that lived in my chest. I had been dealing with heartbreak, disappointment, and a desire for love that felt unmet. Somewhere inside me, I had formed the belief that pain would make me visible. That suffering would cause someone to care, to show up, to stay.

One day, in a moment of emotional fog, I wrote something I didn't fully comprehend:

"Maybe something dramatic would make him see me again."

Those words weren't a prayer.
They weren't a wish.
They weren't even conscious.
But they held emotion.
They held longing.
They held energy.

And energy never returns empty.

I didn't know it then, but I had given the universe a blueprint.

The Moment Everything Shifted

It happened fast. So fast that my mind could barely process the sequence of sounds, movements, and sensations. One moment I was driving, trying to make sense of another heavy day, and the next, everything slowed into a strange silence just before impact. The world outside blurred. My breath caught. My body tightened. And then — The

crash.

Metal folding.
Glass shattering.
My chest thrust forward, then whipped back.
Time bending like it wasn't sure which direction to move.

When everything stopped, I sat still, trembling, surrounded by the remnants of a moment that had already changed me. I wasn't thinking about manifestation or vibration. I wasn't thinking about energy or alignment. I was thinking, "How did this happen? Why today? Why now?"

But something deeper whispered:
You knew.

Not consciously.
But spiritually.

Energetically.

Emotionally.

Somewhere inside, I had already lived this moment because I had created the frequency that brought it into form.

The Awakening That Came Years Later

For years, I told the story the way most people tell their stories:
"It was an accident."
"I was in the wrong place at the wrong time."
"It just happened."

But the more my consciousness expanded, the more I revisited old journals, and the more I reflected on the emotional climate I had been living in during that time, the clearer the truth became.

I had written it.
I had imagined it.
I had felt it.
I had feared it.
I had used it unknowingly as a way to be seen, comforted, validated, or loved.

*And the universe, which responds not to words but to **vibration**, had answered.*

This was not self-blame.
It was self-realization.

The accident wasn't punishment.
It was a mirror reflecting the state of my energy back to me with undeniable clarity.

When you live in emotional scarcity, you attract experiences that match the frequency of scarcity.
When you live in longing, you attract moments that reinforce longing.
When you live in unworthiness, life mirrors back circumstances that echo that belief.

Nothing manifests without your participation — conscious or unconscious.

The Revelation That Changed Everything

Years later, when I fully awakened to the truth of creation, I understood what the accident had actually been:

A manifestation born from a wounded state of being.
A physical consequence of an emotional belief.
A creation of a younger, unaware version of myself.

The accident became one of my greatest teachers because it revealed something I never forgot:

Your energy is creating long before your hands ever touch the physical world.

Every thought carries frequency.
Every emotion carries direction.
Every belief forms structure.

When thought, emotion, and energy align — even unintentionally — they create.

And once I understood that, I also understood this:

If I created from fear, longing, and pain before, then I could create from truth, alignment, and love now.

The accident was not a moment of destruction — it was the doorway to creation.

It taught me the responsibility and power of my own vibration.
It taught me that nothing is random.
It taught me that manifestation is not something you do — it's something you are.

And once you know this, you can no longer pretend you are powerless.

A Practice for Reclaiming Creative Power

Sit with a journal or sit in silence — whichever feels honest.

1. Ask yourself:
"What have I unconsciously created through emotion, fear, or longing?"

2. Write without censoring.
Truth rises when you stop filtering it.

3. Speak this aloud:
"I release the versions of me who created from pain.
I choose to create from truth now."

4. Feel the shift in your body *as the new frequency anchors.*

You are no longer the version of yourself who created from scarcity.

You are awakening into the version that creates from power, intention, clarity, and divine awareness.

The accident was not your downfall.
It was your awakening.
It was the moment your subconscious became visible.
It was the moment you realized the truth:
You've always been the creator. Now you're remembering a conscious one.

Chapter Eleven The Awakening That Won't Let You Go — When Spirit Refuses to Release You Back to Who You Were

Awakening is not a gentle invitation.

It is not a soft whisper you can ignore or a brief moment of clarity you can walk away from.

Awakening is a rupture — a sacred interruption — the moment your soul steps forward and refuses to let your old self keep driving your life.

Once your eyes open, they do not close again.

Not fully.

Not in the same way.

Not without cost.

Awakening is the moment Spirit declares, "You can no longer pretend."

You can no longer numb yourself with old habits.

You can no longer squeeze yourself into old identities. You can no longer stay in rooms where your Spirit no longer fits.

You can no longer return to beliefs that once felt comfortable but now feel suffocating.

Once you see truth, you feel it in everything.

Awakening is not an event — it is a shift in your being.

It rewires you quietly, insistently, relentlessly. It changes the way you hear conversations, the way you sense energy, the way you notice alignment and misalignment in your body. It changes how quickly you recognize when something is off — even when you don't yet have the language for why.

It becomes impossible to stay the same because the old you begins to feel like clothes you outgrew long before you admitted it.

The Irreversible Shift

There comes a moment — sometimes subtle, sometimes explosive — when the new awareness inside you becomes stronger than the old programming you've been carrying. You may not remember the exact second it happened, but you'll remember the feeling.

You'll remember realizing you couldn't return to the version of yourself that apologized for everything, trusted everyone but yourself, dimmed your light to keep peace, or lived small because others felt safer when you shrank.

Awakening pulls you out of that.
It pulls you toward alignment with a force that feels both familiar and brand new.

It pulls you toward the life you were meant to live before the world taught you to shrink.

It pulls you toward choices that honor your soul even when your mind hesitates.

Awakening refuses to release you back to who you were because the old you was built from agreements — not truth.

The new you is built from remembrance.

When Spirit Interrupts Your Life

When awakening begins, Spirit rearranges your life in ways you cannot ignore. People drift. Patterns break. Habits lose their grip. Environments grow uncomfortable. Dreams intensify. Synchronicities multiply. You begin noticing energies you once overlooked, conversations that drain you instantly, and spaces that no longer feel aligned with your Spirit.

At first, all of this can feel like chaos.

You may feel like you're losing control or like your life is falling apart.

But what's actually happening is liberation.

Spirit is clearing what your conscious mind was still clinging to.

Awakening breaks the version of you built from survival so the version of you built from truth can finally emerge.

The Pull You Can't Resist

There is a moment every awakened soul experiences — the point where you realize you are being guided, not gently nudged but pulled. Your life begins to redirect itself with a clarity you didn't ask for but can't ignore.

You feel it in conversations that suddenly feel too small. You feel it in decisions that once felt comfortable but now feel suffocating.
You feel it in your Spirit when you try to go back to the person you used to be — the discomfort is immediate, undeniable, and sharp.

This is Spirit.
This is the awakening refusing to let you go.

It will protect you from the outdated version of yourself.
It will block what diminishes your frequency.
It will remove what you no longer resonate with.
It will close doors that were never meant to open.

Not out of punishment, but out of protection.

Awakening becomes your compass, your boundary, your guide, your truth.

The Awakening Inside the Writing

One of the deepest awakenings of my life happened while writing this book. I didn't expect it, I didn't plan for it, and I certainly didn't sit down thinking Spirit would meet me on the page. But every time I wrote, something inside me shifted — not just mentally, but vibrationally.

As I remembered old stories, old beliefs, and old agreements, I could feel the weight of what I had carried for years begin dissolving. The words didn't feel like they were coming from me — they felt like they were coming through me. My Spirit wasn't just helping me write; it was helping me remember.

There were nights when the writing brought me to tears because I realized I wasn't creating a book — I was recording the truth Spirit had been whispering to me my entire life. I was writing the version of myself I had always been but had never fully allowed myself to become.

The more I wrote, the more impossible it became to return to who I had been before this book.

The more I wrote, the more clearly I heard the guidance I once doubted.

The more I wrote, the more deeply I understood:

This awakening is not temporary. It is who I am.

Writing this book didn't simply tell my story — it transformed me.
It pulled me into alignment.
It exposed old patterns.
It demanded truth.
It revealed purpose.

And once Spirit revealed who I actually am, I could no longer unsee it.

You Cannot Un-Feel What Your Spirit Has Shown You

Once you feel alignment, misalignment becomes unbearable.
Once you taste peace, chaos becomes unbearable.
Once you touch truth, lies become unbearable. Once you meet your higher self, the smaller self becomes unbearable.

Your Spirit refuses to allow you to return to a version of life that contradicts your awakening.

This is why awakened people often say they feel "different." This is why certain relationships dissolve naturally.
This is why certain environments feel heavy instantly. This is why old patterns collapse the moment you try to repeat them.

It is not sensitivity.
It is evolution.

Your soul is rising, and your life is rearranging itself to match your frequency.

A Practice: Listening When Spirit Speaks

Sit in stillness.
Place your hand over your chest.
Slow your breath.
Then ask:
"Where have I outgrown myself?"
"What is Spirit pulling me away from?"
"What can I no longer return to?"

"What truth am I finally ready to live?"

Listen — not in words, but in knowing.

Awakening is not a path you walk back from.
It is a path you rise into.
It is a return to truth.
A return to self.
A return to the divine remembrance that has been waiting for you
all along.

And now that you've awakened… you
will never be the same.

Chapter Twelve
This Was Never Real — Rewriting the Illusion and Inviting the World to Awaken

There comes a point in every awakening where the veil becomes thin — so thin that you can finally see the architecture beneath what you once called reality. Not with your physical eyes, but with the vision of your Spirit, the sense that lives beneath language, beneath memory, beneath the stories you inherited.

This is the moment when you understand, fully and without hesitation, that so much of what you were taught was never true. It was repeated, reinforced, and normalized. But not true. And as you let that truth rise inside you, something in your consciousness clicks into place:

What you called reality was only agreement. What you called truth was only tradition. What you called normal was only programming.

The illusion was never designed to harm you; it was designed to contain you. To keep you small enough to be manageable, obedient enough to be predictable, disconnected enough to be guided by anything but your own divine awareness. But the moment you begin to remember, the moment your frequency rises beyond fear, the structure begins to crumble. Not violently — but inevitably.

Illusion cannot survive the light of awareness.
It dissolves the moment you stop believing in it.

You start to see how deeply the world conditioned you to forget who you are.
You see how shame was used as spiritual discipline.
You see how fear was disguised as wisdom.
You see how guilt was presented as morality.
You see how aging was framed as destiny.
You see how limitation was taught as reality.
You see how suffering was marketed as holiness.

And as each layer falls away, what remains is what has always been there beneath the noise and the teachings and the agreements:
You are not a product of the world. You are a creator within it.

Awakening is not about finding new beliefs.
Awakening is about recognizing the beliefs that never belonged to you in the first place.

As your consciousness expands, you realize that the world you once feared, obeyed, and tried to fit into was built on inherited assumptions — structures held together not by truth, but by collective participation. And the moment you withdraw your participation, the illusion loses its power over your life.

This was never real.

Not in the way you were told.

Not in the way you were trained to perceive it.

And yet, this realization does not produce anger.

It produces compassion.

Because you know now that everyone – from your parents to your teachers to your pastors to your partners – was operating from the level of awareness they had access to. They didn't deceive you. They simply remembered less than you do now.

Your awakening is not a rebellion against them.

It is a remembrance of yourself.

You are not here to condemn what has been.

You are here to rise above it.

This chapter is not about destruction.

It is about clarity.

It is about seeing through the illusion without needing to fight it.

It is about understanding that you do not need to reject the world – you simply need to stop losing yourself inside it.

You have awakened.

And because of that, you are no longer bound by the rules that kept you small.

You are no longer obligated to participate in beliefs that shrink your power.

You are no longer required to accept the destiny someone else wrote for you.

You are free — because you finally remember.

And once remembrance begins, life transforms.
Not instantly.
Not theatrically.
But profoundly.

You begin to speak differently.
You choose differently.
You move differently.
You vibrate differently.
You love yourself differently.
You create differently.

The world responds to you in a new way because you are no longer living inside the illusion — it is now living around you. You become the architect instead of the inhabitant. The witness instead of the follower. The creator instead of the conditioned.

And now, as we reach the end of this book, there is nothing left for me to give you except this:

Question everything you were taught.
Feel everything your Spirit tells you.
And trust the knowing that rises without permission.

Because the world you were handed was an illusion.
But the world you create next will be truth.

This is not the end of your awakening.
This is the beginning of your remembering.

And when you are ready – truly ready – the next book will meet you where you are, not where you were.

I invite you into what comes next.

Because collectively, we change the world.